Unpunctuated
Poetry

Demitria Darby

BookLeaf
Publishing

India | USA | UK

Presentation by *BookLeaf Publishing*

Web: www.bookleafpub.com

E-mail: info@bookleafpub.com

ISBN: 9789363307469

First edition 2022

DEDICATION

This book is dedicated to myself first, for following through, my sons (John and James), my Aunt (Margariette), my Sister (Yolanda) and most importantly these special individuals (Carlos, Carmen, Daneen, Helen, Janise, Katina, Mechelle & Windsday) who gave me a listening ear, as much as needed, to speak freely whenever I chose to share. Thank you...

ACKNOWLEDGEMENT

I would like to give special acknowledgments to "Art in a Fly Space" hosted by Azizi Jasper and Jamal "Dizmantle" Stewart for providing me the opportunity to reconnect with a dormant gift, the gift of Poetry through Spoken Word.

PREFACE

This book formulated from a motivational challenge for myself and others. Many of the poems are derived from personal and fictional experiences, observation and awareness, friendly conversations, historical analysis and the desire to write. It is written to create a rhetorical, interactive thought experience.

This is Your Life

Sometimes we listen to so much instruction
Encounter too many inequities and strife
That these experiences cloud our perspectives
And we forget
This is your life

People impose their thoughts
Their Intellect
Their shortcomings and gains
Although frankly we may have similarities
Our purpose to fulfill may not be quite the same

If you're not mindful
You can become a puppet of suggestions
People seeking to resurrect their lives
Through your lack of ability to demand an
objection

Yes
We all need direction
But at what point do you take the will and show
self reflection
Because it's about you

The world doesn't need a replication
That's why we were made with unique
characteristics
Be explicit
In the authenticity
Of the existence
Of you

Because again
This is your life

You have something to share
Something to discover
Something to give
That will mark your presence here
On this earth

Don't undermine your value
Down play your vision
Or allow yourself to be deterred
Know your worth

Set yourself up to amaze
Because you can
Set yourself up to prosper
Because you will

Live and let learn
Because it's available

Share and expand
Because that's ultimately
The deal

But in all things
Enjoy your time without regret
And never forget
That the natural you is what the world should get

Why

Because

This is your life

Thank you

The Real You

Many times we stray from digging down deep
inside the inner
Strip away that negative stigma of being a sinner
and become a winner

No one can do things better than you
Because no one else is you
But you
Embrace your uniqueness
Express your keenness
And do the best that you can do

Each one of us once had a passionate desire to
be first
We soared against millions
We won
And through the womb we burst

But somehow we have a difficult time recalling
Recalling the greatness that we possess
It's not all your fault you can't remember
The ones before us may have blocked progress

The power is still there
Inside you

Beside you
Just align with you

I need to see it
So we can believe it
So many can achieve it

Display your hidden gift
It's time for a universal shift
We're holding the keys

The keys to unlock the battle within
That society is attempting to spoil
The real you
The real you has that hydraulic oil

You can boost the energy slowing the people
Operating in your gift adds bass to those that
wheeple

Your gift turn locks
Remove rocks
Break through blocks
All the things that hiding it
Will not

In order to bring forth unity
We must connect

And the real you
Has the power to redirect

The real you has a message
The message for a blessing
The blessing to create the spark
The spark to bring light into the dark

The real you speaks to the heart
Changes a dumb mindset to one thinking smart
Sharing your gift is like adding gunpowder to a
dud
It'll penetrate more than just the outside
It reaches the blood

The blood can then carry that seed of exchange
The real you
Manifests
Change

Thank you

What is Perfect

To be perfect means that something is complete
or that there is nothing else to be added
Whatever it is can stand by itself
Alone
It is absolute

But is that really true
Is there no improving within you
Is constant the forever change
Then things are always the same
And evolution is no longer evolution
Because what is now
Shall remain

And this is not so
It raises contradiction to everything we know
There is always room to improve
Which means to be perfect is only the prelude

It's the description of a beginning
A synopsis of the infinite realm we live in
It's the reason why I seek within
To keep perfect in the moment

Because that's all we can do

Perfect exists in snapshot segments of time
It defines what it defines when that period aligns
And changes it's definition
When there is a shift in the paradigm

What was perfect then may not be perfect now
Because information changed
Technology changed
People changed
Even the earth changed

So how can anything be called perfect when
nothing ever stays the same

Thank you

Reminiscent Love

I am awake
I toss and turn because sleep won't let me
Thoughts of you keeps my brain from resting
I'm investing
In us

My mind presses rewind
Over and over and over again
Of yes
Those times
The memories where we toasted and aligned
To merely enjoy the moment

I felt the energy boiling and stirring from the pit
of my stomach
Flying all around my back
Why this type of rush
The kind that resembles a panic attack

My heart throbbing with each beat
Catching a faster rhythm
Breathe I say calmly to myself
Just breathe

But the flutters swimming inside my belly
Won't stop
It's like being tickled with no laughter
Only the will to submit to what I'm feeling
And how I'm feeling
About you
About us

When I think of you
I feel like the earth grows
And widens
To give us more areas to discover
The flowers bloom the uniqueness of colors
Just for us
For lovers

My description is just a depiction of one aspect
Of this season
I thank you for giving me the opportunity
The reason
For sharing a love so pleasing

Thank you

No Matter

No matter the situation
No matter the occupation
I'll always believe in love
It's what makes the world
It's what beautifies a girl
It's like the singing of a white winged dove

When chaos is among us
When hatred divides us
Love is all we need
To strengthen our health
To share our wealth
To create the balance in greed

Love makes me smile
It sparks that inner creative child
It purifies my imagination
I seek to schedule dream vacations
I speak to the ancestors through libations
What a sensation
Love brings

No matter how you perceive it
No matter which ways you receive it
You can't deny that it's the ultimate driving force

It's the energy to keep the marriage
And the lack of that brings divorce
But jump back on course

Love is insatiable
Infectious
To me
The most sought after form of addiction
Place love in any situation
And watch the outcome display
A different depiction

Imagine pouring a Red Bull into the ground
And watching the spirit rise with the energy of
James Brown
That's what positive love can do
For that I am fully committed
Resume fully submitted
And honored to be addicted to you

So
No matter what
Surround me with love
'Cause when the ship sinks
Love makes you float
And eventually I'll be back above

With love
Thank you

The Mask

If we wear a certain type of mask
What is the outcome we seek to get
With Corona
We're told it'll prevent the spread of the virus
But how soon we tend to forget

We breathe through it with such discomfort
Although we placed it on with ease
But does it really matter
When the box says that it doesn't prevent disease

I once heard that the rules were made for the
unjust
So why do we follow this assembly line
The creativity in me makes me do it a different
way
Even though we could have the same objective
in mind

If I do what society does
I'll get what society gets
My life could in turn be all mapped out
With lost opportunities
I'll soon regret

If we choose to wear make up
Is it worn to enhance the beauty of our look
Or is it used as a concealer
To cover up all the bumps and bruises we took

When did we begin to purchase hair
And add it to our face and head
I understand
It makes styling a bit easier
But it changes our natural beauty instead

Our true essence is masked
Covered up and measured by a standard
We unconsciously adopted
Our make up may be flawless
Hairstyle stunning
But chemical poisoning we unfortunately opted

How much do you pay for your mask
How much does it cost to cover your feelings
It's not all monetary
I'm talking emotional dealings

The outcome of "throwing a rock and hiding
your hand" is like living by a double edged
sword
I can learn to suppress my emotions
But am I then cutting my own cord

So to wear a mask
One has to determine whether it's giving you
intrinsic or extrinsic value
Or is it falsely making you someone else
In the end
You'll realize it's so much better when all the
filters are removed
And you can embrace just being your own
natural self

Thank you

Social Distancing

In a time where the world chooses to social
distance
I stand by being close to you
We are connected
Not by what "They Say"
But by what we elect to do

We took this journey to come together
Not for someone or something to disengage that
The purpose is to unite as one
Collectively we prosper
Remember that

Stay away from your family
Naw... the enemy is trying to divide
Stay away from your closest friends
Naw... that's evil in disguise
Stay locked away inside
Naw... I imprison myself as I hide
I don't know what it sounds like to you
But we are being led to our own demise

I vow to stay with you
By your side
Through the darkest of the valleys

Until the moon goes down
And the sun shines light into the darkest alleys
I'll be there
With you
In every rally

We are the connecting source
We not I
Me nor you
But us
Together in unity
Willfully sharing love
That's the formation of in God I trust

Erase the fear
Eradicate the severity of the virus
And live
Live for the continued prosperity of family
Live to bring joy to someone else's life
Live
If it be only just to give

But do so harmoniously
Consciously and aware of source energy
Begin to live animal free
Relinquishing the cruelty of ending a life
Social distance yourself away from that
Cut those ties with your knife

So I say to you
Choose life in every aspect
Distance yourself from negativity
Elect those things that uplift
And bring upon yourself prosperity
Socially accept positivity
Let that be the only space between you and me

Thank you

When There Are No Words

Sometimes I choose not to speak
I haven't formulated the right words
It takes a moment to decipher the messages
I'm listening inside for what I've heard

The pattern
The flow
A combination of words you know
Just placed in a rhythmic state
I've never quite spoken before

Whatever the subject or topic
It must come from within
The stillness helps
To transfer my thoughts through a pen

A quiet place is my Serenity
The sound of air is a form of artwork
It transforms lines into curves
And soon my mind has words

Words and more words
Then the statements align
They keep repeating and repeating
Until most of the sentences rhyme

And as I read what I've written
I enlighten myself
Because these thoughts came to me
With the help of no one else

So when the mouth doesn't speak
Go on the inside for words
The noise that comes from the mind
Allows the pen to write what you've heard

Thank you

Sinless

Scripture says
"He that is without sin cast the first stone upon
her..."
Which means the realm is open
The platform is available
Let her recite and lecture

Our eyes are opened
But shut to the revelation of ourselves
We truly give a picture of what we see
In the reflection of someone else

Why are we blinded to us
Can we look in the mirror and trust
To change our own troublesome mess
The things we speak about less
The experiences we won't confess
Because we too are not sinless

We woke but we sleep
We no longer wade in the shallow
We waist deep

It says
"Judge and be Judged.."

So I'm staring at you
Your sin is no less than my sin
Do we not find this to be true

Our thoughts we manifest
Most defiling all of God's laws
That's why we needed grace
Jesus knew we all had flaws

He died so we could live
And not be condemned for the weakness of our
flesh
He sacrificed HIS life for our future to progress

So why do we keep being bound by measures
that are not the same
When the death of Christ was our symbolic
exchange
Every morning we breathe
Is another opportunity to change

Strike one
Strike two
Strike three
On the third day
HE resurrected for us to see
That HE is the diminisher of stress
HE keeps giving us a new start

Fresh
Sinless

Thank you

Why

When you awaken in the morning
What drives you to climb out of bed
Especially when your body is still restless
And your pillow is comfortably underneath your
head

Why do you get up

Why

What is it that makes you work countless hours
Utilizing your physical strength and maximizing
your mental clarity
Are you really paid your worth
Or are you accepting monetary charity

Why

Why won't you change

Why do we refuse for so long to put a plan in
action
One to our own satisfaction
Breaking barriers of the status quo
Doing consciously what we know

Why aren't we
Exercising a blueprint for a better humanity
One that strengthens our sanity

Why

Because we're guilty
I'm guilty
Of not wanting all the responsibility
Not always forcing one's accountability
To all the possibilities
That tranquility
Can bring into the community

But we can

We can outsmart the system designed to make us
dumb
By quote on quote
"Each one"
"Teach one"
In this season
Plant the seed of reason
Give people a "why"
Encourage them to "try"

Why

Because "We" are the ministers to the people

"We" reach the masses outside the steeple
"We" can connect and empathize with the
forgotten
Place a roadblock to rotten
The spirit that has them stuck
Your voice can wake them up

My people
Speak up

Thank you

Pain

Pain in your life is a turning point
But at that moment it's hard to understand
You question every adverse situation headed
your way
You wonder why you were dealt that hand

It challenges you and opens your eyes
While some lay dormant and stuck
You're thinking to yourself all day and all night
Why have I encountered such bad luck

You call out for God to change this action
But at that time it's just a bit too late
Your path is your path
It's beyond your control
It's nothing we can do about fate

Pain can leave behind some unbearable scars
There's no soap that can wash them away
Sometimes the only thing you can do is cry out
And pray faithfully for a better day

On the outside you still look full
But the inside is hollow and weak
Your reflection in the mirror is a broke glass

A low point
Success is definitely off peak

Every day at this time is a rainy day
Because dry days are still flooded with tears
If you're not conscious of your emotions
Satan will creep in and attempt to exploit your
fears

You'll question the action of the Most High God
Especially if you lose a loved one
But in retrospect it's all in divine order
Because we all pray out to
"Let thy will be done"

Pain makes you change
But your inner strength decides for better or
worse
You can transform that hurt into something
positive
Or it can become your own generational curse

None of us are exempt from pain
And that unfortunate impact made us grow
Some of us may have been hit a bit harder
Because your purpose here may be bigger than
you know

You were punched by Ali but you're still cute
Evander had a mouthpiece but Mike bit him in
dispute
Chris told a joke it was no big deal
Until moments later he was smacked by Will

Physical or emotional
Average individual or a star
Money can't make you exempt
Pain finds you wherever you are

But don't miss the lesson
Limit the awakening
Or squander the chance to mature
There is a message to obtain
A blessing coming
Through everything you managed to endure

So keep moving in love and positivity
Press on even within the deepest of pain
Because once you pull through
You'll realize your life is different
And also that you needed that change

Thank you

Evil Spirits

Evil spirits walk this earth
And they're not presented like you see on tv
They can be handsome
Pretty and humanly shaped
Like you
Like me

They puppet and parade to be your friend
Sucking in all the likeness of your being
Leaches
Lurking for the opportunity
To size you up and do you in

They control the uncontrollable in the mind
Brainwashing you to carry out their will
You know what you're doing is wrong
Right direction is in the heart
But yet you let your action remain ill

Who really has access to you
From which part of this world are you from
Your whole life centers around pleasing
someone else
While your reward is intrinsically
Devaluing and dumb

Evil spirits will trick you
Having you think what you're doing is cool
All the while they're setting you up
To dive head first into a waterless pool

Some hold high office positions
Making you think they are qualified to lead
Many are chosen puppets with ruthless character
flaws
Stand clear of these individuals
I plead

Evil spirited people are host bodies
And actually those individuals are suffering
They bow down to the superficial demonic
world
While good willed intentions are on standby
Buffering

Negative spirits can attack all ages
The question is how do we protect our youth
We tell them the disasters of reckless behaviors
The problems with drinking and drugs
But somehow they don't seem to absorb the truth

Christians say put on the armor of God
Every Witness puts their faith in Jehovah
This demands the need of the Most High God
from the Conscious

While Muslims give all praises to Allah

Everybody has a suggestion
I'll keep faith in the possibility
That eventually the dots will soon connect
To help our youth
And to heal humanity

So for now
Speak the word and spread the word
Use your breath to set yourself free
If you need a scripture remember
James 4:7
"Resist the Devil and he will flee..."

Thank you

Innocently Guilty

I've been guilty of many things
But I still wouldn't change what I do
Many say I'm always looking to find the good in
others
When isn't that what we should all seek too

If I only focus on the negative side of people
Then there's nothing positive for me to see
People tend to forget we have multiple
personalities
Don't just see a limited perspective of me

I am not naive to the offenses of others
Nor do I turn a blind eye to their faults
Finding that good quality in people
That could add to my life
Was the lesson a Great Elder taught

Everyone has some good in them
In spite of the horrific things they may do
Even the worst criminal on the face of this
planet
Took pride in the offenses committed against
you

So if it's bothersome for me to see the good in
people
Then once more convict me like you did above
Because I am innocently guilty again
Guilty of finding that hidden spectrum of love

Thank you

Nature and Me

When I look at nature
I look at me
I begin to visualize
A prophesy

I'm made from you
You're a part of me
We do so much alike
So much I see

I cry tears
You send down rain
I get upset and enraged
Your thunder drives me insane

You need water
I need water too
You clean the air for me
Once I give it to you

We both have our moments
Some in the dark
Some in the light
You keep improving
In spite

Of all the things that might
Try to hinder your beauty
That one sees at sight

You continue to grow
No matter what's around you
No matter the circumstance
You take the chance
And expand

Underneath the rubbish
Underneath the pain
You continue to persevere
Somehow you find a lane

You branch out in different ways
I network to do the same
You ascend upward
I reach higher
Mutually I comprehend
We both desire
You yield produce
I humanly reproduce
I grow you feed
Thanks for nourishing my seed

You are my root chakra
You lay the foundation

Everyday forward
We seek elevation

It seems so general
And you supply every mineral
So why did I cheat
With this processed freak
Who led the deceit
That constantly defeats
Our bond

A substitute from nature does not compare
We chase the dollar and chose health care
We used to live for hundreds of years
Now that's rare
From the hospital windows
Millions now stare

They left you
You never left us
You sent herbs through the weeds
But they fertilized your seed
Recklessly controlling the earth
Like pills attempt to eliminate birth
Now we all suffer for forgetting your worth

You are valuable and most necessarily important
We need you
To continue to unselfishly help the nation

While we multiply generations
To live from your manifestations
And the visible creation
You portray
Of God's salvation

You are the Mother to the world
Land to land
Sea to sea
I thank you for displaying
Everything about nature and me

We rise when we honor her
Fail when we disrespect her
Live healthy when we eat from her
Prosper when we protect her
Love better when we love her
So learn to value who she is
She is her
Nature...

Thank you

Youthful Coaching Seed

One of the most influential moments of being a
coach is to get a child to believe
You take a seed and plant it deep
Watering it with every possible scenario until
That child can manage to perceive

That foundational concept must be repetitive
Like learning a multiplication chart
Keep reinforcing the basics
Until that youthful mind has a grounded place to
start

In the moment
Children may find it hard to process
They're hearing the words but unaware
A coach once hollered all the time to us
"You're the best thing out there"

As players we joked and laughed
Not knowing how that seed would manifest
But as the season progressed
We bought into that statement
And began to believe we were the best

That time was magical
It shifted our mindset and uplifted our self
esteem
We saw that we could achieve so much
We knew dreams were not just dreams

So never think your words fall upon deaf ears
Keep speaking life until you break that curse
Because once you penetrate the seat of the soul
You'll understand how much your effort was
worth

Thank you

Stand Down or Up

A round of applause for Colin Kaepernick
And again for Kyrie Irving
They kneeled down and stood up for things they
believed in
While receiving backlash
So undeserving

I thought this was a free country
Who's mandating right or wrong
Men of such an elite stature
But a gesture of egalitarianism
Let's you know you don't belong

It doesn't matter you have money
Your riches only mean so much
In the eyes of some
You do as I say
Or bear the consequences of not doing such

Even now as we are here today
There's talk about the war between Russia and
Ukraine
Why is there a disparity of treatment for
melanated people

When everyone is desperately seeking survival
the same

Color is still the embedded bottom line
Even though we believe we've evolved so far
The invisible line is still there to let you know
That nothing can alter who you are

You are the source of The Creator
Your inside manifests the outside
Think better
Love more
See the future you'd like to live
And uplift the environment where you reside

Love is the ultimate solution
To the revolution
Of our journey
Anytime one rises against
We must all strongly support thee

There stands to me
Is considered as Oprah would put it
"One of the whispers of the universe"
A signal to express more love and compassion
If we want to see change immerse

Pay closer attention to acts "For the People"
And less to Immoral distractions

One creates emotional balance
While the other results in stressful bodily actions

So reset your thoughts and focus on what is
needed
That being
The spread of love
Any revolutionary action is a reminder that you
are entitled to greatness
By our Creator above

Thank you

Which Way

If only there was an arrow
To point the right direction in the road to take
If only there was a printed blueprint to each and
every step we take

If only I could reach you telepathically
You would know then just how I feel
If only you had opened your heart
To let love flourish the whole ordeal

If only you had broken the bondage
The bondage of the barriers that held you back
If only you had taken more moments
To smell the roses along the track

If only I had recognized the game
The one involving grand larceny theft
Then it would've been easy to pick the road to
the right
Because I would've known sooner
You were headed left

Thank you

Sisters

What do you do with the pain and hurt
What do you do with the deceit
Why do we except such shortcomings
When we know it leads straight to defeat

It's not that you are stupid
Desperate or in despair
A wolf can spot a gentle heart
And pray on the fact that you care

Stop lowering yourself to revenge
Be thankful that you can feel
The anguish that they carry inside
Is not measurable to a person that's real

He couldn't see your worth
But God knew all the time
Stop trying to set his ass on fire
When the Lord said "Vengeance is Mine"

Walk without regret
You had a lessen to learn
Strike a match to ignite yourself
And let that broken bridge burn

Sisters you are so much more
Despite how things may seem
Put on your crown
And stand up tall
Bring back that Beautiful Queen

It was a very very dark moment
But obviously now you know
No one can dim the light you possess
When God gave it to you to glow

So don't waste another hour
Turn the lock and bolt the door
You've been living in lack too long
You're about to be blessed with more

Pain is only temporary
Strength is built within
Get up and go about your life
You're a daughter of the Most High my friend

Thank you

Time

When the pressure of time is among us
How do you respond
Does your mind focus to execute
Or does your dreams float away
Like lily pads in a pond

Time holds for no one
Absorb the moment and utilize the minutes to
expand
Expand happiness
Expand positivity
Expand love
And watch the increase in your internal equity

If it's true that we don't attract what we want
We attract who we are
Then
To have an abundance of wealth
Shouldn't we clean up our inner health

Health is wealth
We've heard that a million times yet we suppress
it subconsciously
Bring that into fruition
And maximize your life fruitfully

As time continues to tick
We still must make choices
Choices that lead to a better us
Choices that express our voices

Do we face our challenges and persevere
through whatever outcome
Or do we accept
A dead destiny
By not pursuing the dream of your heart
You follow a pattern truly beneath thee

Time is the only race we have
Because our biological meter is humanly
unknown
And whether or not you truly run up your tab
Can only be measured when your gone

How much of your time is wasted with
Procrastination
Frustration
Wrong occupations
And acrimonious relations

Only you know

Time is our most precious asset
Yet we carelessly disregard its worth
Distracted by our action to entertain foolery

While chipping away the wholeness
Of a dream to birth

Time is of the essence
A powerful
Redundantly used statement
But so true
Time waits for no one
Not me
Not you

So I ask you
What are you doing with your time
And what contribution to humanity have you
added
To your own personal lifeline

Because time is time

Thank you

Attitude

What type of an attitude do you have
What do you see reflective in you
Are you calm in conflict resolution
Or do you blow up if people blow up towards
you

Where did this behavior come from
How did you know how to respond
What are the thoughts embedded on the inside
How did you formulate this bond

Are your actions a combination of family
Are you influenced by where you live
Were you trained in some sort of a facility
Or is it the attention to the tv and music you give

Was it due to the absence or presence of love
Was it the surroundings of violent or nonviolent
actions
Was there a witnessing of disparity or fairness of
treatment
Was there a standard to the event and the
prompted reaction

Were you ever part of a gang
Were you raised in a religious setting
I'm just asking the questions
That could possibly lead to the attitudes we're
getting

Do you act from some sort of desperation
Or are you operating from contentment
Are you satisfied with who you are
Or are you harboring some inner resentment

How do you treat your body
Are you conscious of what you eat
Could it be that what's introduced into the small
intestine is related to how one thinks

Did you suffer any childhood trauma
Better yet did you manage to overcome
Is it possible that you have not broken the cycle
Are you repeating what's already been done

Are you the product of a recycled past
Or are you rebuilding by breaking the chain
It's documented that when you do something
new
You fire off different neurons in the brain

Our attitudes are Indicative
They tell a story like the numbers to the credit
score
If you don't find some type of balance in life
Your attitude may possibly display the burdens
you bore

Now tell me do you think this is fair
Certain circumstances have shielded us from
you
But all of it brought you into alignment
Just allow your volcanic expression of greatness
to flow through

So know that I'm not calling you overly cheerful
I'm not even calling you rude
What I'm asking is that you become mindful of
your experiences
Because whether you know it or not
It's shaping your attitude

Thank you

Think it and Speak it

What is really going on
What is it that everyone sees
People are leaving the earth in numbers
Chem trails are killing the trees

Who can you really trust
Love blinds you over to lust
A temper flare
Shots in the air
Ash to ash
Now dust to dust

What can we do to change
The elders are preaching the same
Chemical chronic is ruining our youth
Low dopamine
Slowing the brain

Everyone's in a hurry
Not focusing on loving yourself
Surgery
Pills
Injections
Now look
Oh my God you're somebody else

If no one ever told you then listen
You are beautiful and uniquely made
If you're misunderstood so be it
Don't attach their negative shade

Christians are losing their faith
And why 'cause you're spiritually safe
If Calvary was here
Then why do you fear
Hypocrisy has no place

I'm thinking it
So I'm speaking it
Releasing it
To find some peace in it
No longer unsure
I struggle no more
Some things just can't be ignore

Many have lost their way
Their vaping from day to day
It's blackening their lungs
It's aging their lungs
All wrong
But who am I to say

Negativity is killing humanity
Poor thinking is causing insanity

Health issues resulting from vanity
Who changed how we were designed to be

Oh yeah I forgot to mention
How covid is causing division
United we're strong
Social distanced alone
Another soldier picked off and gone

We're smarter than how we're acting
We keep allowing them to practice
You followed the instructions you read
You did what it was they said
But somehow your loved one still dead
Now tell me who's being mislead

Grandma had every remedy
Without any diploma or PHD
They trained us while we were in school
To become this educated fool
We hardened our ears to truth
Don't listen
No certificate of proof

Now who will you choose to follow
Your circle of knowledge is hollow
Keep relying on everyone else
When the answers are inside yourself

None of what I said is a secret
We circle these thoughts on a frequent
You heard it again from her
Who
That artist
Demitria
Umm

Thank you